A long time
I dream
All over the world,
And often I'd ask about the past
Driving everyone crazy fast!
Amused by this my parents thought,
Why not call me "History" for short?

Little Miss HISTORY Travels to
LA BREA TAR PITS & MUSEUM
© 2017 Barbara Ann Mojica. All Rights Reserved.

Published in The UNITED STATES of AMERICA by
eugenus STUDIOS, LLC
P.O. BOX 112
CRARYVILLE, NY 12521
E-Mail: Barbara@LittleMissHistory.com,
WebSite: www.LittleMissHISTORY.com

ISBN-13: 9780988503083
ISBN-10: 0988503085

Dedicated to
JESSIE LOUGHRAN,
my godmother

BARBARA ANN MOJICA'S

Little Miss
HISTORY ®

Travels
to

LA BREA
TAR
PITS
& MUSEUM

Illustrated by VICTOR RAMON MOJICA

The La Brea Tar Pits are in the Miracle Mile section of Los Angeles, California, a city of almost four million people.

LA BREA TAR PITS Prehistoric-fossil excavation site 5801 Wilshire Blvd. Los Angeles, CA 90036 (213) 763-3499

Los Angeles

The La Brea Tar Pits and Hancock Park were once part of a Mexican land grant called Rancho La Brea.

Brea is the Spanish word for tar.
The black goo (tar) is actually asphalt,
the heavy part of crude oil.

This part of Los Angeles sits about one thousand feet above an oil field. The pressure in the rocks below pushes oil up through cracks.

Asphalt then forms small pools when it rises to the top.

Herbivores, plant-eating animals, seeking vegetation stepped into these asphalt pools getting stuck.

Carnivores, meat-eaters, were also trapped when they tried to eat animals stuck in the pools of goo. Other animals arrived and the cycle continued over and over.

The Observation Pit at La Brea opened in 1952 as its first museum.

In the pit, visitors can see fossils of these herbivores and carnivores piled onto each other in a pool of asphalt.

In 1969, Paleontologists began
a new dig at La Brea, Pit 91.

Fossils found in the top twelve feet are about twenty-eight thousand years old. Those found below twelve feet are about forty thousand years old.

In a laboratory at La Brea, nicknamed the Fish Bowl, scientists carefully clean, identify and record the fossils.

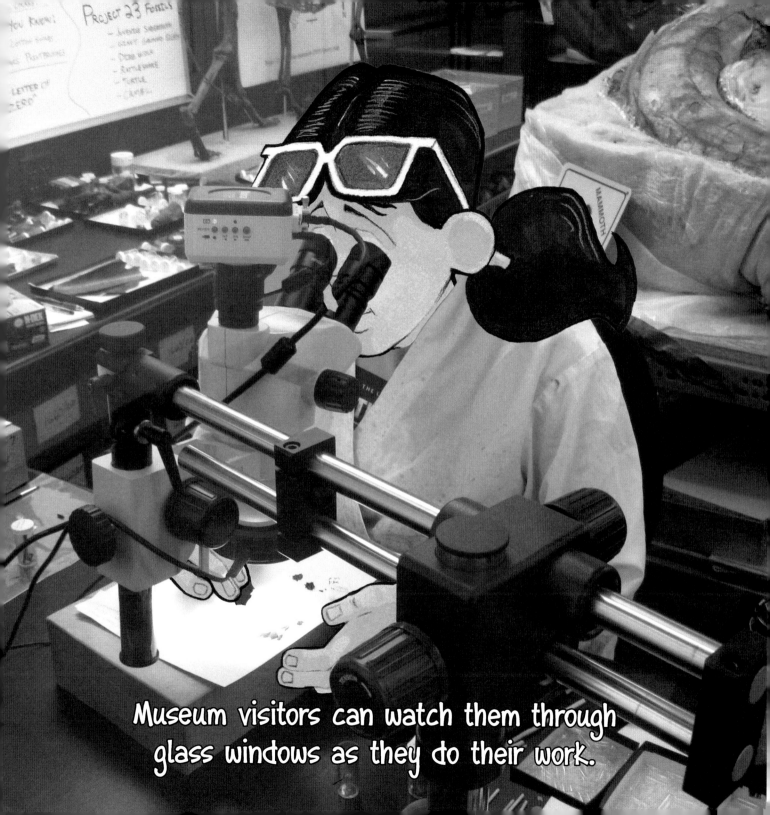

Museum visitors can watch them through glass windows as they do their work.

In 1875, William Denton, a geologist/paleontologist, first recognized that the animal remains were fossils.

He made this observation while visiting the Hancock family asphalt mine at Rancho La Brea, as it was known back then.

By 1905, W.W. Orcutt had discovered skulls at La Brea of a saber-toothed cat, dire wolf, and ground sloth fossils.

John C. Merriam, in 1909, organized the first scientific excavations at La Brea. His student Chester Stock drew up a plan to display fossils at the site.

George Allan Hancock inherited Rancho La Brea from his father, Captain Henry Hancock. The oil discovered there made him wealthy. He donated twenty-three acres to Los Angeles in 1916, later called Hancock Park. He wished to preserve and display the fossils discovered at La Brea.

The National Parks Service designated Rancho La Brea a National Natural Landmark in 1963.

George C. Page hitchhiked to Los Angeles at age twelve with only two dollars and thirty cents in his pocket. He worked hard and saved his money.

One Christmas, he sent his family a gift package of California fruit. That inspired him to start a business shipping fruit all over the country.

One day George Page heard the rumors about fossils in the tar pits and envisioned a museum.

George C. Page died in 2000, just shy of his one-hundredth birthday.

LOS ANGELES COUNTY
MUSEUM OF NATURAL HISTORY

GEORGE C. PAGE MUSEUM

BOARD OF SUPERVISORS · COUNTY OF LOS ANGELES
EDMUND D. EDELMAN

PETER F. SCHABARUM   JAMES A. HAYES
KENNETH HAHN   BAXTER WARD

HARRY L. HUFFORD   STEPHEN J. KOONCE
Chief Administrative Officer   Director, Facilities Department

Dr. GILES W. MEAD   THORNTON, FAGAN, A.I.A. & Associates
Director, Museum of Natural History   Architect

GEORGE C. PAGE   SAMUELSON, WESTON CONSTRUCTORS
Donor   Builder

BOARD OF GOVERNORS

FRANKLIN OTIS BOOTH JR.   DAVID W. HEARST
RICHARD CALL, M.D.   NORMAN O. HOUSTON
MRS. JUSTIN DART   DOUGLAS J. MACDONALD
WILLIAM W. DREWRY JR.   CHARLES O. MATCHAM
C.V. DUFF   RICHARD C. SEAVER
ALFRED M. ESBERG   MYNATT SMITH
WILLIAM M. GARLAND, II   MRS. E. HADLEY STUART JR.
ED N. HARRISON   JOHN G. WIGMORE
LEWIS J. HASTINGS   DR. M. NORVEL YOUNG

1977

Today visitors marvel at his achievement.

Step beyond these glass
doors into the lobby of
this wonderful museum
and travel back in time
thousands of years.

Gaze upward at the huge mounted skeletons of fossils.

Walk outside into the
Pleistocene Age Garden
based on the plant
fossils discovered at
La Brea.

See for yourself how tough it is to escape the tar pits at the Tar Pulling Station.

When you do take your trip back in time, just be careful walking around. Watch out for those asphalt seeps!

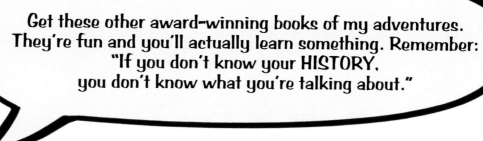

GLOSSARY
WORDS TO KNOW

ASPHALT - a black, sticky substance obtained from natural deposits in the earth.

CARNIVORES - animals that eat other animals.

ENVISION - imagine as a future possibility.

EXCAVATION - a large hole made by digging.

FOSSILS - remains of a living thing from a former age.

GEOLOGIST - a scientist who studies earth's physical structure and its history.

HERBIVORES - animals that eat plants.

MAMMALS - animals that are warm-blooded with a backbone. They feed their young milk and have skin covered with hair or fur.

PALEONTOLOGIST - a scientist who studies fossil animals and plants.

PLEISTOCENE ICE AGE - time when most of the earth was covered in ice, roughly 40.000 to 10,000 years ago.

SEEPS - places where liquid oozes slowly through the ground.

TAR - dark thick liquid from wood or coal.

VEGETATION - all the plants living in a certain place.

Made in the
USA
Columbia, SC